LANGUAGE·OF·FLOWERS

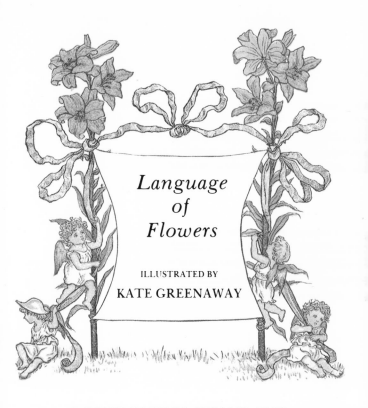

Language
of
Flowers

ILLUSTRATED BY
KATE GREENAWAY

DOVER PUBLICATIONS, INC.
New York

This Dover edition, first published in 1992, is an unabridged
republication of the edition published by George Routledge and
Sons, London, n.d.

Manufactured in the United States of America
Dover Publications, Inc., 31 East 2nd Street, Mineola, N.Y. 11501

Library of Congress Cataloging-in-Publication Data

Greenaway, Kate, 1846–1901.
    Language of flowers / illustrated by Kate Greenaway.
        p.   cm.
    Originally published: London : Routledge, 1884.
    ISBN 0-486-27372-5 (pbk.)
    1. Flower language. 2. Flowers—Poetry. I. Title.
GR780.G72 1990
398'.368213—dc20
                                        92-30765
                                          CIP

Abecedary	. . .	*Volubility.*
Abatina	. . .	*Fickleness.*
Acacia	. . .	*Friendship.*
Acacia, Rose or White	.	*Elegance.*
Acacia, Yellow	. .	*Secret love.*
Acanthus	. . .	*The fine arts. Artifice.*
Acalia	. . .	*Temperance.*
Achillea Millefolia	.	*War.*
Aconite (Wolfsbane)	.	*Misanthropy.*
Aconite, Crowfoot	.	*Lustre.*
Adonis, Flos	. .	*Painful recollections.*
African Marigold	. .	*Vulgar minds.*
Agnus Castus	. .	*Coldness. Indifference.*
Agrimony	. . .	*Thankfulness. Gratitude.*
Almond (Common)	.	*Stupidity. Indiscretion.*

Almond (Flowering) . .	*Hope.*
Almond, Laurel . .	*Perfidy*
Allspice	*Compassion.*
Aloe	*Grief. Religious superstition.*
Althæa Frutex (Syrian Mallow) . . .	*Persuasion.*
Alyssum (Sweet) . .	*Worth beyond beauty.*
Amaranth (Globe) . .	*Immortality. Unfading love.*
Amaranth (Cockscomb) .	*Foppery. Affectation.*
Amaryllis . . .	*Pride. Timidity. Splendid beauty.*
Ambrosia . . .	*Love returned.*
American Cowslip . .	*Divine beauty.*
American Elm . .	*Patriotism.*
American Linden . .	*Matrimony.*
American Starwort . .	*Welcome to a stranger. Cheerfulness in old age.*
Amethyst . . .	*Admiration.*
Anemone (Zephyr Flower)	*Sickness. Expectation.*
Anemone (Garden). .	*Forsaken.*
Angelica . . .	*Inspiration.*
Angrec	*Royalty.*
Apple	*Temptation.*
Apple (Blossom) . .	*Preference. Fame speaks him great and good.*
Apple, Thorn . .	*Deceitful charms.*
Apocynum (Dog's Vane) .	*Deceit.*
Arbor Vitæ . . .	*Unchanging Friendship. Live for me.*
Arum (Wake Robin) .	*Ardour.*
Ash-leaved Trumpet Flower .	*Separation.*
Ash Tree . . .	*Grandeur.*
Aspen Tree . . .	*Lamentation.*
Aster (China) . . .	*Variety. Afterthought.*
Asphodel . . .	*My regrets follow you to the grave.*
Auricula . . .	*Painting.*
Auricula, Scarlet . .	*Avarice.*
Austurtium . . .	*Splendour.*
Azalea	*Temperance.*

Bachelor's Buttons	.	.	.	*Celibacy.*
Balm	.	.	.	*Sympathy.*
Balm, Gentle	.	.	.	*Pleasantry.*
Balm of Gilead	.	.	.	*Cure. Relief.*
Balsam, Red	,	.	.	*Touch me not. Impatient resolves.*
Balsam, Yellow	.	.	.	*Impatience.*
Barberry	.	.	.	*Sourness of temper.*
Barberry Tree	.	.	.	*Sharpness.*
Basil	.	.	.	*Hatred.*
Bay Leaf	.	.	.	*I change but in death.*
Bay (Rose) Rhododendron	.	*Danger. Beware.*
Bay Tree	.	.	.	*Glory.*
Bay Wreath	.	.	.	*Reward of merit.*
Bearded Crepis	.	.	.	*Protection.*
Beech Tree	.	.	.	*Prosperity.*
Bee Orchis	.	.	.	*Industry.*
Bee Ophrys	.	.	.	*Error.*
Belladonna	.	.	.	*Silence.*
Bell Flower, Pyramidal	.	*Constancy.*
Bell Flower (small white)	.	*Gratitude.*

Belvedere	*I declare against you.*
Betony	*Surprise.*
Bilberry	*Treachery.*
Bindweed, Great . .	*Insinuation.*
Bindweed, Small . .	*Humility.*
Birch	*Meekness.*
Birdsfoot Trefoil . .	*Revenge.*
Bittersweet; Nightshade	*Truth.*
Black Poplar . . .	*Courage.*
Blackthorn . . .	*Difficulty.*
Bladder Nut Tree . .	*Frivolity. Amusement.*
Bluebottle (Centaury) .	*Delicacy.*
Bluebell	*Constancy.*
Blue-flowered Greek Valerian	*Rupture.*
Borus Henricus . .	*Goodness.*
Borage	*Bluntness.*
Box Tree . . .	*Stoicism.*
Bramble	*Lowliness. Envy. Remorse.*
Branch of Currants .	*You please all.*
Branch of Thorns . .	*Severity. Rigour.*
Bridal Rose . . .	*Happy love.*
Broom	*Humility. Neatness.*
Buckbean . . .	*Calm repose.*
Bud of White Rose .	*Heart ignorant of love.*
Bugloss	*Falsehood.*
Bulrush	*Indiscretion. Docility.*
Bundle of Reeds, with their Panicles . . .	*Music.*
Burdock	*Importunity. Touch me not.*
Buttercup (Kingcup) .	*Ingratitude. Childishness.*
Butterfly Orchis . .	*Gaiety.*
Butterfly Weed . .	*Let me go.*

Cabbage	.	.	.	.	.	*Profit.*
Cacalia	.	.	.	.	.	*Adulation.*
Cactus	.	.	.	.	.	*Warmth.*
Calla Æthiopica	.	.	.	.	*Magnificent Beauty.*
Calycanthus	.	.	.	.	*Benevolence.*
Camellia Japonica, Red	.	.	*Unpretending excellence.*
Camellia Japonica, White	.	*Perfected loveliness.*
Camomile	.	.	.	.	*Energy in adversity.*
Canary Grass	.	.	.	.	*Perseverance.*
Candytuft	.	.	.	*	*Indifference.*
Canterbury Bell	.	.	.	*Acknowledgement.*
Cape Jasmine	.	.	.	*I'm too happy.*
Cardamine	.	.	.	.	*Paternal error.*
Carnation, Deep Red	.	.	*Alas! for my poor heart.*
Carnation, Striped	.	.	.	*Refusal.*
Carnation, Yellow	.	.	.	*Disdain.*

11

Cardinal Flower . .	.	*Distinction.*
Catchfly . . .	.	*Snare.*
Catchfly, Red .	.	*Youthful love.*
Catchfly, White .	.	*Betrayed.*
Cedar . . .	.	*Strength.*
Cedar of Lebanon .	.	*Incorruptible.*
Cedar Leaf . .	.	*I live for thee.*
Celandine (Lesser) .	.	*Joys to come.*
Cereus (Creeping) .	.	*Modest genius.*
Centaury . . .	.	*Delicacy.*
Champignon . .	.	*Suspicion.*
Chequered Fritillary .	.	*Persecution.*
Cherry Tree . .	.	*Good education.*
Cherry Tree, White .	.	*Deception.*
Chesnut Tree . .	.	*Do me justice. Luxury.*
Chickweed . .	.	*Rendezvous.*
Chicory . . .	.	*Frugality.*
China Aster . .	.	*Variety.*
China Aster, Double .	.	*I partake your sentiments.*
China Aster, Single .	.	*I will think of it.*
China or Indian Pink .	.	*Aversion.*
China Rose . .	.	*Beauty always new.*
Chinese Chrysanthemum .	.	*Cheerfulness under adversity.*
Christmas Rose . .	.	*Relieve my anxiety.*
Chrysanthemum, Red .	.	*I love.*
Chrysanthemum, White .	.	*Truth.*
Chrysanthemum, Yellow .	.	*Slighted love.*
Cinquefoil . .	.	*Maternal affection.*
Circæa . . .	.	*Spell.*
Cistus, or Rock Rose .	.	*Popular favour.*
Cistus, Gum . .	.	*I shall die to-morrow.*
Citron . . .	.	*Ill-natured beauty.*
Clematis . . .	.	*Mental beauty.*
Clematis, Evergreen .	.	*Poverty.*
Clotbur . . .	.	*Rudeness. Pertinacity.*
Cloves . . .	.	*Dignity.*
Clover, Four-leaved .	.	*Be mine.*
Clover, Red . .	.	*Industry.*
Clover, White . .	.	*Think of me.*
Cobæa , . .	.	*Gossip.*
Cockscomb Amaranth .	.	*Foppery. Affectation. Singularity.*

Colchicum, or Meadow Saffron	My best days are past.
Coltsfoot	Justice shall be done.
Columbine	Folly.
Columbine, Purple	Resolved to win.
Columbine, Red	Anxious and trembling.
Convolvulus	Bonds.
Convolvulus, Blue (Minor)	Repose. Night.
Convolvulus, Major	Extinguished hopes.
Convolvulus, Pink	Worth sustained by judicious and tender affection.
Corchorus	Impatient of absence.
Coreopsis	Always cheerful.
Coreopsis Arkansa	Love at first sight.
Coriander	Hidden worth.
Corn	Riches.
Corn, Broken	Quarrel.
Corn Straw	Agreement.
Corn Bottle	Delicacy.
Corn Cockle	Gentility.
Cornel Tree	Duration.
Coronella	Success crown your wishes.
Cowslip	Pensiveness. Winning grace.
Cowslip, American	Divine beauty. You are my divinity.
Cranberry	Cure for heartache.
Creeping Cereus	Horror.
Cress	Stability. Power.
Crocus	Abuse not.
Crocus, Spring	Youthful gladness.
Crocus, Saffron	Mirth.
Crown Imperial	Majesty. Power.

13

Crowsbill	. . . .	*Envy.*
Crowfoot	. . . .	*Ingratitude.*
Crowfoot (Aconite-leaved)	.	*Lustre.*
Cuckoo Plant	. . .	*Ardour.*
Cudweed, American	.	*Unceasing remembrance.*
Currant	. . . .	*Thy frown will kill me.*
Cuscuta	. . . .	*Meanness.*
Cyclamen	. . . .	*Diffidence.*
Cypress	. . . .	*Death. Mourning.*

Daffodil	*Regard.*
Dahlia	*Instability.*
Daisy	*Innocence.*
Daisy, Garden . .	*I share your sentiments*
Daisy, Michaelmas .	*Farewell.*
Daisy, Party-coloured .	*Beauty.*
Daisy, Wild . . .	*I will think of it.*
Damask Rose . . .	*Brilliant complexion.*
Dandelion . . .	*Rustic oracle.*
Daphne Odora . .	*Painting the lily.*
Darnel (Ray grass). .	*Vice*
Dead Leaves . . .	*Sadness.*
Dew Plant . . .	*A Serenade.*
Dittany of Crete . .	*Birth.*
Dittany of Crete, White .	*Passion.*
Dock	*Patience.*
Dodder of Thyme . .	*Baseness.*
Dogsbane . . .	*Deceit. Falsehood.*
Dogwood . . .	*Durability.*
Dragon Plant . . .	*Snare.*
Dragonwort . . .	*Horror.*
Dried Flax . . .	*Utility.*

Ebony Tree	.	.	.	*Blackness.*
Eglantine (Sweetbrier)	.	.		*Poetry. I wound to heal.*
Elder	.	.	.	*Zealousness.*
Elm	.	.	.	*Dignity.*
Enchanter's Nightshade	.			*Witchcraft. Sorcery.*
Endive	.	.	.	*Frugality.*
Eupatorium	.	.		*Delay.*
Everflowering Candytuft	.			*Indifference.*
Evergreen Clematis	.			*Poverty.*
Evergreen Thorn	.	.		*Solace in adversity.*
Everlasting	.	.	.	*Never-ceasing remembrance.*
Everlasting Pea	.	.		*Lasting pleasure.*

Fennel	.	.	.	.	*Worthy all praise. Strength.*
Fern	.	.	.	.	*Fascination.*
Ficoides, Ice Plant	.	.			*Your looks freeze me.*
Fig	.	.	.	.	*Argument.*
Fig Marigold	.	.	.		*Idleness.*
Fig Tree	.	.	.		*Prolific.*
Filbert	.	.	.		*Reconciliation*
Fir	.	.	.	.	*Time.*
Fir Tree	.	.	.		*Elevation.*
Flax	.	.	.	.	*Domestic Industry. Fate.*
					I feel your kindness.
Flax-leaved Goldy-locks		.			*Tardiness.*
Fleur-de-Lis	.	.	.		*Flame. I burn.*
Fleur-de-Luce	.	.	.		*Fire.*
Flowering Fern	.	.			*Reverie.*
Flowering Reed	.	.			*Confidence in Heaven.*
Flower-of-an-Hour	.	.			*Delicate beauty.*
Fly Orchis	.	.	.		*Error.*

Flytrap	.	.	.	.	*Deceit.*
Fool's Parsley	.	.	*Silliness.*
Forget Me Not	.	.	*True love. Forget me not.*
Foxglove	.	.	.	*Insincerity.*
Foxtail Grass	.	.	.	*Sporting.*
French Honeysuckle	.	.	*Rustic beauty.*
French Marigold	.	.	*Jealousy.*
French Willow	.	.	*Bravery and humanity.*
Frog Ophrys	.	.	.	*Disgust.*
Fuller's Teasel	.	.	*Misanthropy.*
Fumitory	.	.	.	*Spleen.*
Fuchsia, Scarlet	.	.	*Taste.*

Garden Anemone	.	.	.	Forsaken.
Garden Chervil	.	.	.	Sincerity.
Garden Daisy	.	.	.	I partake your sentiments.
Garden Marigold	.	.	.	Uneasiness.
Garden Ranunculus	.	.	You are rich in attractions.
Garden Sage	.	.	.	Esteem.
Garland of Roses	.	.	Reward of virtue.
Germander Speedwell	.	Facility.
Geranium, Dark	.	.	Melancholy.
Geranium, Ivy	.	.	.	Bridal favour.
Geranium, Lemon	.	.	Unexpected meeting.
Geranium, Nutmeg	.	Expected meeting.
Geranium, Oak-leaved	.	True friendship.
Geranium, Pencilled	.	Ingenuity.
Geranium, Rose-scented	.	Preference.
Geranium, Scarlet	.	.	Comforting. Stupidity.
Geranium, Silver-leaved	.	Recall.
Geranium, Wild	.	.	Steadfast piety.

Gillyflower	.	.	.	*Bonds of affection.*
Glory Flower	.	.	.	*Glorious beauty.*
Goat's Rue	.	.	.	*Reason.*
Golden Rod	.	.	.	*Precaution.*
Gooseberry	.	.	.	*Anticipation.*
Gourd	.	.	.	*Extent. Bulk.*
Grape, Wild	.	.	.	*Charity.*
Grass	.	.	.	*Submission. Utility.*
Guelder Rose	.	.	.	*Winter. Age.*

Hand Flower Tree	.	.	.	*Warning.*
Harebell	.	.	.	*Submission. Grief.*
Hawkweed	.	.	.	*Quicksightedness.*
Hawthorn	.	.	.	*Hope.*
Hazel	.	.	.	*Reconciliation.*
Heath	.	.	.	*Solitude.*
Helenium	.	.	.	*Tears.*
Heliotrope	.	.	.	*Devotion. Faithfulness.*
Hellebore	.	.	.	*Scandal. Calumny.*
Helmet Flower (Monkshood).				*Knight-errantry.*
Hemlock	.	.	.	*You will be my death.*
Hemp	.	.	.	*Fate.*
Henbane	.	.	.	*Imperfection.*
Hepatica	.	.	.	*Confidence.*
Hibiscus	.	.	.	*Delicate beauty.*
Holly	.	.	.	*Foresight.*
Holly Herb	.	.	.	*Enchantment.*
Hollyhock	.	.	.	*Ambition. Fecundity.*
Honesty	.	.	.	*Honesty. Fascination.*

Honey Flower	. .	*Love sweet and secret.*
Honeysuckle .	. .	*Generous and devoted affection.*
Honeysuckle Coral	.	*The colour of my fate.*
Honeysuckle (French)	.	*Rustic beauty.*
Hop .	. .	*Injustice.*
Hornbeam	. .	*Ornament.*
Horse Chesnut	. .	*Luxury.*
Hortensia	. .	*You are cold.*
Houseleek	. .	*Vivacity. Domestic industry.*
Houstonia	. .	*Content.*
Hoya .	. .	*Sculpture.*
Humble Plant	. .	*Despondency.*
Hundred-leaved Rose	.	*Dignity of mind.*
Hyacinth .	. .	*Sport. Game. Play.*
Hyacinth, White .	.	*Unobtrusive loveliness.*
Hydrangea .	. .	*A boaster. Heartlessness.*
Hyssop .	. .	*Cleanliness.*

Iceland Moss	*Health.*
Ice Plant . . .	*Your looks freeze me*
Imperial Montague . .	*Power.*
Indian Cress	*Warlike trophy.*
Indian Jasmine (Ipomœa) .	*Attachment.*
Indian Pink (Double) . .	*Always lovely.*
Indian Plum . . .	*Privation.*
Iris	*Message.*
Iris, German . . .	*Flame.*
Ivy	*Fidelity. Marriage.*
Ivy, Sprig of, with tendrils .	*Assiduous to please.*

Jacob's Ladder	.	.	.	*Come down.*
Japan Rose	.	.	.	*Beauty is your only attraction.*
Jasmine	.	.	.	*Amiability.*
Jasmine, Cape	.	.	*Transport of joy.*
Jasmine, Carolina	.	.	*Separation.*
Jasmine, Indian	.	.	*I attach myself to you.*
Jasmine, Spanish	.	.	*Sensuality.*
Jasmine, Yellow	.	.	*Grace and elegance.*
Jonquil	.	.	.	*I desire a return of affection.*
Judas Tree	.	.	.	*Unbelief. Betrayal.*
Juniper	.	.	.	*Succour. Protection.*
Justicia	.	.	.	*The perfection of female loveliness.*

Kennedia . . . . Mental Beauty.
King-cups . . . . Desire of Riches.

Laburnum	.	.	.	*Forsaken. Pensive Beauty.*
Lady's Slipper	.	.	.	*Capricious Beauty. Win me and wear me.*
Lagerstræmia, Indian	.			*Eloquence.*
Lantana	.	.	.	*Rigour.*
Larch	.	.	.	*Audacity. Boldness.*
Larkspur	.	.	.	*Lightness. Levity.*
Larkspur, Pink	.		.	*Fickleness.*
Larkspur, Purple	.	.		*Haughtiness.*
Laurel	.	.	.	*Glory.*
Laurel, Common, in flower	.			*Perfidy.*
Laurel, Ground	.	.		*Perseverance.*
Laurel, Mountain	.	.		*Ambition.*
Laurel-leaved Magnolia	.			*Dignity.*
Laurestina	.	.	.	*A token. I die if neglected.*
Lavender	.	.	.	*Distrust.*
Leaves (dead)	.	.		*Melancholy.*
Lemon	.	.	.	*Zest.*
Lemon Blossoms	.	.		*Fidelity in love.*
Lettuce	.	.	.	*Cold-heartedness.*
Lichen	.	.	.	*Dejection. Solitude.*

Lilac, Field	.	.	*Humility.*
Lilac, Purple	.	.	*First emotions of love.*
Lilac, White	.	.	*Youthful Innocence.*
Lily, Day	.	.	*Coquetry.*
Lily, Imperial	.	.	*Majesty.*
Lily, White	.	.	*Purity. Sweetness.*
Lily, Yellow	.	.	*Falsehood. Gaiety.*
Lily of the Valley	.	.	*Return of happiness.*
Linden or Lime Trees	.	.	*Conjugal love.*
Lint	.	.	*I feel my obligations.*
Live Oak	.	.	*Liberty.*
Liverwort	.	.	*Confidence.*
Licorice, Wild	.	.	*I declare against yon.*
Lobelia	.	.	*Malevolence.*
Locust Tree	.	.	*Elegance.*
Locust Tree (green)	.	.	*Affection beyond the grave.*
London Pride	.	.	*Frivolity.*
Lote Tree	.	.	*Concord.*
Lotus	.	.	*Eloquence.*
Lotus Flower	.	.	*Estranged love.*
Lotus Leaf	.	.	*Recantation.*
Love in a Mist	.	.	*Perplexity.*
Love lies Bleeding	.	.	*Hopeless, not heartless.*
Lucern	.	.	*Life.*
Lupine	.	.	*Voraciousness. Imagination.*

Madder	Calumny.
Magnolia . . .	Love of Nature.
Magnolia, Swamp . .	Perseverance.
Mallow	Mildness.
Mallow, Marsh . .	Beneficence.
Mallow, Syrian . .	Consumed by love.
Mallow, Venetian . .	Delicate beauty.
Manchineal Tree . .	Falsehood.
Mandrake . . .	Horror.
Maple	Reserve.
Marigold. . . .	Grief.
Marigold, African . .	Vulgar minds.
Marigold, French . .	Jealousy.
Marigold, Prophetic .	Prediction.
Marigold and Cypress .	Despair.
Marjoram . . .	Blushes.
Marvel of Peru . .	Timidity.

Meadow Lychnis	. .	*Wit.*
Meadow Saffron	. .	*My best days are past.*
Meadowsweet	. .	*Uselessness.*
Mercury	. .	*Goodness.*
Mesembryanthemum	. .	*Idleness.*
Mezereon	. .	*Desire to please.*
Michaelmas Daisy	. .	*Afterthought.*
Mignionette	. .	*Your qualities surpass your charms.*
Milfoil	. .	*War.*
Milkvetch	. .	*Your presence softens my pains.*
Milkwort	. .	*Hermitage.*
Mimosa (Sensitive Plant)	.	*Sensitiveness.*
Mint	. .	*Virtue.*
Mistletoe	. .	*I surmount difficulties.*
Mock Orange	. .	*Counterfeit.*
Monkshood (Helmet Flower)	.	*Chivalry. Knight-errantry.*
Moonwort	. .	*Forgetfulness.*
Morning Glory	. .	*Affectation.*
Moschatel	. .	*Weakness.*
Moss	. .	*Maternal love.*
Mosses	. .	*Ennui.*
Mossy Saxifrage	. .	*Affection.*
Motherwort	. .	*Concealed love.*
Mountain Ash	. .	*Prudence.*
Mourning Bride	. .	*Unfortunate attachment. I have lost all.*
Mouse-eared Chickweed	.	*Ingenuous simplicity.*
Mouse-eared Scorpion Grass	.	*Forget me not.*
Moving Plant	. .	*Agitation.*
Mudwort	. .	*Tranquillity.*
Mugwort	. .	*Happiness.*
Mulberry Tree (Black)	.	*I shall not survive you.*
Mulberry Tree (White)	.	*Wisdom.*
Mushroom	. .	*Suspicion.*
Musk Plant	. .	*Weakness.*
Mustard Seed	. .	*Indifference.*
Myrobalan	. .	*Privation.*
Myrrh	. .	*Gladness.*
Myrtle	. .	*Love.*

Narcissus . . .	*Egotism.*
Nasturtium . . .	*Patriotism.*
Nettle, Burning . .	*Slander.*
Nettle Tree . . .	*Concert.*
Night-blooming Cereus .	*Transient beauty.*
Night Convolvulus .	*Night.*
Nightshade . .	*Truth.*

Oak Leaves	.	.	.	*Bravery.*
Oak Tree	.	.	.	*Hospitality.*
Oak (White)	.	.	.	*Independence.*
Oats	.	.	.	*The witching soul of music.*
Oleander	.	.	.	*Beware.*
Olive	.	.	.	*Peace.*
Orange Blossoms	.	.	*Your purity equals your loveliness.*
Orange Flowers	.	.	*Chastity. Bridal festivities.*
Orange Tree	.	.	*Generosity.*
Orchis	.	.	.	*A Belle.*
Osier	.	.	.	*Frankness.*
Osmunda	.	.	.	*Dreams.*
Ox Eye	.	.	.	*Patience.*

Palm	.	.	.	.	.	*Victory.*
Pansy	.	.	.	.	.	*Thoughts.*
Parsley	.	.	.	.	.	*Festivity.*
Pasque Flower	.	.	.	*You have no claims.*
Passion Flower	.	.	.	*Religious superstition.*
Patience Dock	.	.	.	*Patience.*
Pea, Everlasting	.	.	*An appointed meeting. Lasting Pleasure.*
Pea, Sweet	.	.	.	.	*Departure.*
Peach	.	.	.	.	*Your qualities, like your charms, are unequalled.*
Peach Blossom	.	.	.	*I am your captive.*
Pear	.	.	.	.	.	*Affection.*
Pear Tree	.	.	.	.	*Comfort.*
Pennyroyal	.	.	.	.	*Flee away.*
Peony	.	.	.	.	.	*Shame. Bashfulness.*
Peppermint	.	.	.	.	*Warmth of feeling.*
Periwinkle, Blue	.	.	*Early friendship.*
Periwinkle, White	.	.	*Pleasures of memory.*
Persicaria	.	.	.	.	*Restoration.*

Persimon	*Bury me amid Nature's beauties.*
Peruvian Heliotrope . .	*Devotion.*
Pheasant's Eye . . .	*Remembrance.*
Phlox	*Unanimity.*
Pigeon Berry . . .	*Indifference.*
Pimpernel . . .	*Change. Assignation.*
Pine	*Pity.*
Pine-apple . . .	*You are perfect.*
Pine, Pitch . . .	*Philosophy.*
Pine, Spruce . . .	*Hope in adversity.*
Pink	*Boldness.*
Pink, Carnation . .	*Woman's love.*
Pink, Indian, Double .	*Always lovely.*
Pink, Indian, Single .	*Aversion.*
Pink, Mountain . .	*Aspiring.*
Pink, Red, Double .	*Pure and ardent love.*
Pink, Single . .	*Pure love.*
Pink, Variegated . .	*Refusal.*
Pink, White . . .	*Ingeniousness. Talent.*
Plane Tree . . .	*Genius.*
Plum, Indian . . .	*Privation.*
Plum Tree . . .	*Fidelity.*
Plum, Wild . . .	*Independence.*
Polyanthus . . .	*Pride of riches.*
Polyanthus, Crimson .	*The heart's mystery.*
Polyanthus, Lilac . .	*Confidence.*
Pomegranate . . .	*Foolishness.*
Pomegranate, Flower .	*Mature elegance.*
Poplar, Black . .	*Courage.*
Poplar, White . .	*Time.*
Poppy, Red . . .	*Consolation.*
Poppy, Scarlet . .	*Fantastic extravagance.*
Poppy, White . .	*Sleep. My bane. My antidote.*
Potato	*Benevolence.*

Prickly Pear	.	.	.	*Satire.*
Pride of China	.	.	.	*Dissension.*
Primrose	.	.	.	*Early youth.*
Primrose, Evening	.	.	*Inconstancy.*
Primrose, Red	.	.	*Unpatronized merit.*
Privet	.	.	.	*Prohibition.*
Purple Clover	.	.	.	*Provident.*
Pyrus Japonica	.	.	*Fairies' fire.*

Quaking-Grass	*Agitation.*
Quamoclit .	*Busybody.*
Queen's Rocket . . .	*You are the queen of*
	coquettes. Fashion.
Quince	*Temptation.*

Ragged Robin	.	.	.	*Wit.*
Ranunculus	.	.	.	*You are radiant with charms.*
Ranunculus, Garden	.	.	*You are rich in attractions.*
Ranunculus, Wild	.	.	*Ingratitude.*
Raspberry	.	.	.	*Remorse.*
Ray Grass	.	.	.	*Vice.*
Red Catchfly	.	.	.	*Youthful love.*
Reed	.	.	.	*Complaisance. Music.*
Reed, Split	.	.	.	*Indiscretion.*
Rhododendron (Rosebay)	.	*Danger. Beware.*
Rhubarb	.	.	.	*Advice.*
Rocket	.	.	.	*Rivalry.*
Rose	.	.	.	*Love.*
Rose, Austrian	.	.	*Thou art all that is lovely.*
Rose, Bridal	.	.	*Happy love.*
Rose, Burgundy	.	.	*Unconscious beauty.*
Rose, Cabbage	.	.	*Ambassador of love.*
Rose, Campion	.	.	*Only deserve my love.*
Rose, Carolina	.	.	*Love is dangerous.*
Rose, China	.	.	*Beauty always new.*
Rose, Christmas	.	.	*Tranquillize my anxiety.*

Rose, Daily . . .	*Thy smile I aspire to.*
Rose, Damask . .	*Brilliant complexion.*
Rose, Deep Red . .	*Bashful shame.*
Rose, Dog . . .	*Pleasure and pain.*
Rose, Guelder . .	*Winter. Age.*
Rose, Hundred-leaved .	*Pride.*
Rose, Japan . . .	*Beauty is your only attraction.*
Rose, Maiden Blush .	*If you love me, you will find it out.*
Rose, Multiflora . .	*Grace.*
Rose, Mundi . . .	*Variety.*
Rose, Musk . . .	*Capricious beauty.*
Rose, Musk, Cluster .	*Charming.*
Rose, Single . . .	*Simplicity.*
Rose, Thornless . .	*Early attachment.*
Rose, Unique . . .	*Call me not beautiful.*
Rose, White . . .	*I am worthy of you.*
Rose, White (withered) .	*Transient impressions.*
Rose, Yellow . . .	*Decrease of love. Jealousy.*
Rose, York and Lancaster .	*War.*
Rose, Full-blown, placed over two Buds . . .	*Secrecy.*
Rose, White and Red together. . . .	*Unity.*
Roses, Crown of . .	*Reward of virtue.*
Rosebud, Red . .	*Pure and lovely.*
Rosebud, White . .	*Girlhood.*
Rosebud, Moss . .	*Confession of love.*
Rosebay (Rhododendron) .	*Beware. Danger.*
Rosemary . . .	*Remembrance.*
Rudbeckia . . .	*Justice.*
Rue	*Disdain.*
Rush	*Docility.*
Rye Grass . . .	*Changeable disposition*

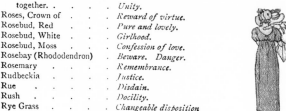

Saffron	.	.	.	.	Beware of excess.
Saffron Crocus	.	.	.	Mirth.
Saffron, Meadow	.	.	.	My happiest days are past.
Sage	.	.	.	.	Domestic virtue.
Sage, Garden	.	.	.	Esteem.
Sainfoin	.	.	.	.	Agitation.
Saint John's Wort	.	.	Animosity. Superstition.
Sardony	.	.	.	.	Irony.
Saxifrage, Mossy	.	.	Affection.
Scabious	.	.	.	.	Unfortunate love.
Scabious, Sweet	.	.	Widowhood.
Scarlet Lychnis	.	.	Sunbeaming eyes.
Schinus	.	.	.	.	Religious enthusiasm.
Scotch Fir	.	.	.	Elevation.
Sensitive Plant	.	.	Sensibility. Delicate feelings.
Senvy	.	.	.	.	Indifference.
Shamrock	.	.	.	Light heartedness.
Snakesfoot	.	.	.	Horror.

Snapdragon	*Presumption.*
Snowball	*Bound.*
Snowdrop	*Hope.*
Sorrel	*Affection.*
Sorrel, Wild	*Wit ill-timed.*
Sorrel, Wood	*Joy.*
Southernwood	*Jest. Bantering.*
Spanish Jasmine	*Sensuality.*
Spearmint	*Warmth of sentiment.*
Speedwell	*Female fidelity.*
Speedwell, Germander	*Facility.*
Speedwell, Spiked	*Semblance.*
Spider, Ophrys	*Adroitness.*
Spiderwort	*Esteem not love.*
Spiked Willow Herb	*Pretension.*
Spindle Tree	*Your charms are engraven on my heart.*
Star of Bethlehem	*Purity.*
Starwort	*Afterthought.*
Starwort, American	*Cheerfulness in old age.*
Stock	*Lasting beauty.*
Stock, Ten Week	*Promptness.*
Stonecrop	*Tranquillity.*
Straw, Broken	*Rupture of a contract.*
Straw, Whole	*Union.*
Strawberry Tree	*Esteem and love.*
Sumach, Venice	*Splendour. Intellectual excellence.*
Sunflower, Dwarf	*Adoration.*
Sunflower, Tall	*Haughtiness.*
Swallow-wort	*Cure for heartache.*
Sweet Basil	*Good wishes.*
Sweetbrier, American	*Simplicity.*
Sweetbrier, European	*I wound to heal.*
Sweetbrier, Yellow	*Decrease of love.*
Sweet Pea	*Delicate pleasures.*
Sweet Sultan	*Felicity.*
Sweet William	*Gallantry.*
Sycamore	*Curiosity.*
Syringa	*Memory.*
Syringa, Carolina	*Disappointment.*

Tamarisk	.	.	.	Crime.
Tansy (Wild).	.	.		*I declare war against you*
Teasel	.	.	.	*Misanthropy.*
Tendrils of Climbing Plants				*Ties.*
Thistle, Common	.	.		*Austerity.*
Thistle, Fuller's	.	.		*Misanthropy*
Thistle, Scotch	.	.		*Retaliation.*
Thorn Apple	.	.		*Deceitful charms.*
Thorn, Branch of	.	.		*Severity.*
Thrift	.	.	.	*Sympathy.*
Throatwort	.	.		*Neglected beauty.*
Thyme.	.	.	.	*Activity.*
Tiger Flower	.	.		*For once may pride befriend me.*
Traveller's Joy	.	.		*Safety.*
Tree of Life	.	.		*Old age.*
Trefoil.	.	.	.	*Revenge.*

Tremella Nestoc	. .	*Resistance.*
Trillium Pictum	. .	*Modest beauty.*
Truffle . .	. .	*Surprise.*
Trumpet Flower	. .	*Fame.*
Tuberose .	. .	*Dangerous pleasures.*
Tulip . .	. .	*Fame.*
Tulip, Red .	. .	*Declaration of love.*
Tulip, Variegated .	. .	*Beautiful eyes.*
Tulip, Yellow	. .	*Hopeless love.*
Turnip . .	. .	*Charity.*
Tussilage (Sweet-scented)	.	*Justice shall be done you.*

Valerian . . .	.	*An accommodating*
		disposition.
Valerian, Greek .	.	*Rupture.*
Venice Sumach .	.	*Intellectual excellence*
		Splendour.
Venus' Car . .	.	*Fly with me.*
Venus' Looking-glass	.	*Flattery.*
Venus' Trap . .	.	*Deceit.*
Vernal Grass . .	.	*Poor, but happy.*
Veronica . . .	.	*Fidelity.*
Vervain . . .	.	*Enchantment.*
Vine . . .	.	*Intoxication.*
Violet, Blue . .	.	*Faithfulness.*
Violet, Dame . .	.	*Watchfulness.*
Violet, Sweet . .	.	*Modesty.*
Violet, Yellow . .	.	*Rural happiness.*
Virginian Spiderwort	.	*Momentary happiness.*
Virgin's Bower . .	.	*Filial love.*
Volkamenia . .	.	*May you be happy.*

Walnut	.	.	.	Intellect. Stratagem.
Wall-flower	.	.	.	Fidelity in adversity.
Water Lily	.	.	.	Purity of heart.
Water Melon	.	.	.	Bulkiness.
Wax Plant	.	.	.	Susceptibility.
Wheat Stalk	.	.	.	Riches.
Whin	.	.	.	Anger.
White Jasmine	.	.	.	Amiableness.
White Lily	.	.	.	Purity and Modesty.
White Mullein	.	.	.	Good nature.
White Oak	.	.	.	Independence.
White Pink	.	.	.	Talent.
White Poplar	.	.	.	Time.
White Rose (dried)	.	.	.	Death preferable to loss of innocence.
Whortleberry	.	.	.	Treason.
Willow, Creeping	.	.	.	Love forsaken.
Willow, Water	.	.	.	Freedom.

Willow, Weeping	.	.	.	*Mourning.*
Willow-Herb	.	.	.	*Pretension.*
Willow, French	.	.	.	*Bravery and humanity.*
Winter Cherry	.	.	.	*Deception.*
Witch Hazel	.	.	.	*A spell.*
Woodbine	.	.	.	*Fraternal love.*
Wood Sorrel	.	.	.	*Joy. Maternal tenderness.*
Wormwood	.	.	.	*Absence.*

| Xanthium | . | . | . | . | *Rudeness. Pertinacity.* |
| Xeranthemum | . | . | . | *Cheerfulness under adversity.* |

Yew . . . . . *Sorrow*

| Zephyr Flower | . | . | . | *Expectation.* |
| Zinnia | . | . | . | . | *Thoughts of absent friends* |

Absence	. . . . .	*Wormwood.*
Abuse not	. . . .	*Crocus.*
Acknowledgment	. . . .	*Canterbury Bell.*
Activity	. . . .	*Thyme.*
Admiration	. . . .	*Amethyst.*
Adoration	. . . .	*Dwarf Sunflower*
Adroitness	. . . .	*Spider Ophrys.*
Adulation	. . . .	*Cacalia.*
Advice	. . . .	*Rhubarb.*
Affection	. . . .	*Mossy Saxifrage.*
Affection	. . . .	*Pear.*
Affection	. . . .	*Sorrel.*
Affection beyond the grave	. .	*Green Locust.*
Affection, maternal	. .	*Cinquefoil.*
Affectation	. . . .	*Cockscomb Amaranth.*
Affectation	. . . .	*Morning Glory.*
Affectation	. . . .	*Michaelmas Daisy.*
Afterthought	. . . .	*Starwort.*
Afterthought	. . . .	*China Aster.*
Afterthought	. . . .	*Straw.*
Agreement	. . . .	*Guelder Rose.*
Age	. . . .	*Moving Plant.*
Agitation	. . . .	*Sainfoin.*
Agitation	. . . .	*Deep Red Carnation.*
Alas! for my poor heart	. .	*Coreopsis.*
Always cheerful	. . . .	*Indian Pink (double).*
Always lovely	. . . .	*Cabbage Rose.*
Ambassador of love	. . . .	*Cabbage Rose.*

Amiability	*Jasmine.*
Anger	*Whin.*
Animosity	*St. John's Wort.*
Anticipation	*Gooseberry.*
Anxious and trembling	*Red Columbine.*
Ardour	*Cuckoo Plant.*
Argument	*Fig.*
Arts or artifice	*Acanthus.*
Assiduous to please	*Sprig of Ivy with tendrils.*
Assignation	*Pimpernel.*
Attachment	*Indian Jasmine.*
Audacity	*Larch.*
Avarice	*Scarlet Auricula.*
Aversion	*China or Indian Pink.*
Bantering	*Southernwood.*
Baseness	*Dodder of Thyme.*
Bashfulness	*Peony.*
Bashful shame	*Deep Red Rose.*
Beautiful eyes	*Variegated Tulip.*
Beauty	*Party-coloured Daisy.*
Beauty always new	*China Rose.*
Beauty, capricious	*Lady's Slipper.*
Beauty, capricious	*Musk Rose.*
Beauty, delicate	*Flower of an Hour.*
Beauty, delicate	*Hibiscus.*
Beauty, divine	*American Cowslip.*
Beauty, glorious	*Glory Flower.*
Beauty, lasting	*Stock.*
Beauty, magnificent	*Calla Æthiopica.*
Beauty, mental	*Clematis.*
Beauty, modest	*Trillium Pictum.*
Beauty, neglected	*Throatwort.*
Beauty, pensive	*Laburnum.*
Beauty, rustic	*French Honeysuckle.*
Beauty, unconscious	*Burgundy Rose.*
Beauty is your only attraction	*Japan Rose.*
Belle	*Orchis.*
Be mine	*Four-leaved Clover.*
Beneficence	*Marshmallow.*
Benevolence	*Potato.*
Betrayed	*White Catchfly.*
Beware	*Oleander.*
Beware	*Rosebay.*
Blackness	*Ebony Tree.*
Bluntness	*Borage.*
Blushes	*Marjoram.*
Boaster	*Hydrangea.*
Boldness	*Pink.*
Bonds	*Convolvulus.*

49

Bonds of Affection	*Gillyflower.*
Bravery	*Oak Leaves.*
Bravery and humanity	*French Willow.*
Bridal favour	*Ivy Geranium.*
Brilliant complexion	*Damask Rose.*
Bulk	*Water Melon. Gourd.*
Busybody	*Quamoclit.*
Bury me amid Nature's beauties	*Persimon.*
Call me not beautiful	*Rose Unique.*
Calm repose	*Buckbean.*
Calumny	*Hellebore.*
Calumny	*Madder.*
Change	*Pimpernel.*
Changeable disposition	*Rye Grass.*
Charity	*Turnip.*
Charming	*Cluster of Musk Roses.*
Charms, deceitful	*Thorn Apple.*
Cheerfulness in old age	*American Starwort.*
Cheerfulness under adversity	*Chinese Chrysanthemum.*
Chivalry	*Monkshood (Helmet Flower).*
Cleanliness	*Hyssop.*
Coldheartedness	*Lettuce.*
Coldness	*Agnus Castus.*
Colour of my life	*Coral Honeysuckle.*
Come down	*Jacob's Ladder.*
Comfort	*Pear Tree.*
Comforting	*Scarlet Geranium.*
Compassion	*Allspice.*
Concealed love	*Motherwort.*
Concert	*Nettle Tree.*
Concord	*Lote Tree.*
Confession of love	*Moss Rosebud.*
Confidence	*Hepatica.*
Confidence	*Lilac Polyanthus.*
Confidence	*Liverwort.*
Confidence in Heaven	*Flowering Reed.*
Conjugal love	*Lime, or Linden Tree.*
Consolation	*Red Poppy.*
Constancy	*Bluebell.*
Consumed by love	*Syrian Mallow.*
Counterfeit	*Mock Orange.*
Courage	*Black Poplar.*
Crime	*Tamarisk.*
Cure	*Balm of Gilead.*
Cure for heartache	*Swallow-wort.*
Curiosity	*Sycamore.*
Danger	*Rhododendron. Rosebay.*
Dangerous Pleasures	*Tuberose.*

Death	*Cypress.*
Death preferable to loss of innocence . .	*White Rose (dried).*
Deceit	*Apocynum.*
Deceit	*Flytrap.*
Deceit	*Dogsbane.*
Deceitful charms	*Thorn Apple.*
Deception	*White Cherry Tree.*
Declaration of love	*Red Tulip.*
Decrease of love	*Yellow Rose.*
Delay	*Eupatorium.*
Delicacy	*Bluebottle. Centaury.*
Dejection	*Lichen.*
Desire to please	*Mezereon.*
Despair	*Cypress.*
Despondency	*Humble Plant.*
Devotion	*Peruvian Heliotrope.*
Difficulty	*Blackthorn.*
Dignity	*Cloves.*
Dignity	*Laurel-leaved Magnolia.*
Disappointment	*Carolina Syringa.*
Disdain	*Yellow Carnation.*
Disdain	*Rue.*
Disgust	*Frog Ophrys.*
Dissension	*Pride of China.*
Distinction	*Cardinal Flower.*
Distrust	*Lavender.*
Divine beauty	*American Cowslip.*
Docility	*Rush.*
Domestic industry	*Flax.*
Domestic virtue	*Sage.*
Durability	*Dogwood.*
Duration	*Cornel Tree.*
Early attachment	*Thornless Rose*
Early friendship	*Blue Periwinkle.*
Early youth	*Primrose.*
Elegance	*Locust Tree.*
Elegance and grace	*Yellow Jasmine.*
Elevation	*Scotch Fir.*
Eloquence	*Indian Lagerstræmia.*
Enchantment	*Holly Herb.*
Enchantment	*Vervain.*
Energy in adversity	*Camomile.*
Envy	*Bramble.*
Error	*Bee Ophrys.*
Error	*Fly Orchis.*
Esteem	*Garden Sage.*
Esteem not love	*Spiderwort.*
Esteem and love	*Strawberry Tree.*
Estranged love	*Lotus Flower.*

Excellence	*Camellia Japonica.*
Expectation	*Anemone.*
Expectation	*Zephyr Flower.*
Expected meeting	*Nutmeg Geranium.*
Extent	*Gourd.*
Extinguished hopes	*Major Convolvulus.*
Facility	*Germander Speedwell.*
Fairies' fire	*Pyrus Japonica.*
Faithfulness	*Blue Violet.*
Faithfulness	*Heliotrope.*
Falsehood	*Buglass.*
Falsehood	*Yellow Lily.*
Falsehood	*Manchineal Tree.*
Fame	*Tulip. Trumpet Flower.*
Fame speaks him great and good	*Apple Blossom.*
Fantastic extravagance	*Scarlet Poppy.*
Farewell	*Michaelmas Daisy.*
Fascination	*Fern.*
Fascination	*Honesty.*
Fashion	*Queen's Rocket.*
Fecundity	*Hollyhock.*
Felicity	*Sweet Sultan.*
Female fidelity	*Speedwell.*
Festivity	*Parsley.*
Fickleness	*Abatina.*
Fickleness	*Pink Larkspur.*
Filial love	*Virgin's bower.*
Fidelity	*Veronica. Ivy.*
Fidelity	*Plum Tree.*
Fidelity in adversity	*Wall-flower.*
Fidelity in love	*Lemon Blossoms.*
Fire	*Fleur-de-Luce.*
First emotions of love	*Purple Lilac.*
Flame	*Fleur-de-lis. Iris.*
Flattery	*Venus' Looking-glass.*
Flee away	*Pennyroyal.*
Fly with me	*Venus' Car.*
Folly	*Columbine.*
Foppery	*Cockscomb Amaranth.*
Foolishness	*Pomegranate.*
Foresight	*Holly.*
Forgetfulness	*Moonwort.*
Forget me not	*Forget Me Not.*
For once may pride befriend me	*Tiger Flower.*
Forsaken	*Garden Anemone.*
Forsaken	*Laburnum.*
Frankness	*Osier.*
Fraternal love	*Woodbine.*
Freedom	*Water Willow.*

Freshness	*Damask Rose.*
Friendship	*Acacia.*
Friendship, early	*Blue Periwinkle.*
Friendship, true	*Oak-leaved Geranium.*
Friendship, unchanging	*Arbor Vitæ.*
Frivolity	*London Pride.*
Frugality	*Chicory. Endive.*
Gaiety	*Butterfly Orchis.*
Gaiety	*Yellow Lily.*
Gallantry	*Sweet William.*
Generosity	*Orange Tree.*
Generous and devoted affection	*French Honeysuckle.*
Genius	*Plane Tree.*
Gentility	*Corn Cockle.*
Girlhood	*White Rosebud.*
Gladness	*Myrrh.*
Glory	*Bay Tree.*
Glory	*Laurel.*
Glorious beauty	*Glory Flower.*
Goodness	*Bonus Henricus.*
Goodness	*Mercury.*
Good education	*Cherry Tree.*
Good wishes	*Sweet Bazil.*
Goodnature	*White Mullein.*
Gossip	*Cobœa.*
Grace	*Multiflora Rose.*
Grace and elegance	*Yellow Jasmine.*
Grandeur	*Ash Tree.*
Gratitude	*Small White Bell-flower.*
Grief	*Harebell.*
Grief	*Marigold.*
Happy love	*Bridal Rose.*
Hatred	*Basil.*
Haughtiness	*Purple Larkspur.*
Haughtiness	*Tall Sunflower.*
Health	*Iceland Moss.*
Hermitage	*Milkwort.*
Hidden worth	*Coriander.*
Honesty	*Honesty.*
Hope	*Flowering Almond.*
Hope	*Hawthorn.*
Hope	*Snowdrop.*
Hope in adversity	*Spruce Pine.*
Hopeless love	*Yellow Tulip.*
Hopeless, not heartless	*Love Lies Bleeding.*
Horror	*Mandrake.*
Horror	*Dragonswort.*
Horror	*Snakesfoot.*

Hospitality	Oak Tree.
Humility	Broom.
Humility	Small Bindweed.
Humility	Field Lilac.
I am too happy	Cape Jasmine.
I am your captive	Peach Blossom.
I am worthy of you	White Rose.
I change but in death	Bay Leaf.
I declare against you	Belvedere.
I declare against you	Liquorice.
I declare war against you . . .	Wild Tansy.
I die if neglected	Laurestina.
I desire a return of affection . .	Jonquil.
I feel my obligations	Lint.
I feel your kindness	Flax.
I have lost all	Mourning Bride.
I live for thee	Cedar Leaf.
I love	Red Chrysanthemum.
I partake of your sentiments . .	Double China Aster.
I partake your sentiments . . .	Garden Daisy.
I shall die to-morrow	Gum Cistus.
I shall not survive you . . .	Black Mulberry.
I surmount difficulties	Mistletoe.
I will think of it	Single China Aster.
I will think of it	Wild Daisy.
I wound to heal	Eglantine (Sweetbrier).
If you love me, you will find it out .	Maiden Blush Rose.
Idleness	Mesembryanthemum.
Ill-natured beauty	Citron.
Imagination	Lupine.
Immortality	Amaranth (Globe).
Impatience	Yellow Balsam.
Impatient of absence	Corchorus.
Impatient resolves	Red Balsam.
Imperfection	Henbane.
Importunity	Burdock.
Inconstancy	Evening Primrose.
Incorruptible	Cedar of Lebanon.
Independence	Wild Plum Tree.
Independence	White Oak.
Indifference	Everflowering Candytuft.
Indifference	Mustard Seed.
Indifference	Pigeon Berry.
Indifference	Senvy.
Indiscretion	Split Reed.
Industry	Red Clover.
Industry, Domestic	Flax.
Ingeniousness	White Pink.
Ingenuity	Pencilled Geranium.

Ingenuous simplicity	Mouse-eared Chickweed.
Ingratitude	Crowfoot.
Innocence	Daisy.
Insincerity	Foxglove.
Insinuation	Great Bindweed.
Inspiration	Angelica.
Instability	Dahlia.
Intellect	Walnut.
Intoxication	Vine.
Irony	Sardony.
Jealousy	French Marigold.
Jealousy	Yellow Rose.
Jest	Southernwood.
Joy	Wood Sorrel.
Joys to come	Lesser Celandine.
Justice	Rudbeckia.
Justice shall be done to you	Coltsfoot.
Justice shall be done to you	Sweet-scented Tussilage.
Knight-errantry	Helmet Flower (Monkshood).
Lamentation	Aspen Tree.
Lasting beauty	Stock.
Lasting pleasures	Everlasting Pea.
Let me go	Butterfly Weed.
Levity	Larkspur.
Liberty	Live Oak.
Life	Lucern.
Lightheartedness	Shamrock.
Lightness	Larkspur.
Live for me	Arbor Vitæ.
Love	Myrtle.
Love	Rose.
Love, forsaken	Creeping Willow.
Love, returned	Ambrosia.
Love is dangerous	Carolina Rose.
Lustre	Aconite-leaved Crowfoot, or Fair Maid of France.
Luxury	Chesnut Tree.
Magnificent beauty	Calla Æthiopica.
Majesty	Crown Imperial.
Malevolence	Lobelia.
Marriage	Ivy.
Maternal affection	Cinquefoil.
Maternal love	Moss.
Maternal tenderness	Wood Sorrel.
Matrimony	American Linden.
May you be happy	Volkamenia.

Meanness	*Cuscuta.*
Meekness	*Birch.*
Melancholy	*Dark Geranium.*
Melancholy	*Dead Leaves.*
Mental beauty	*Clematis.*
Mental beauty	*Kennedia.*
Message	*Iris.*
Mildness	*Mallow.*
Mirth	*Saffron Crocus.*
Misanthropy.	*Aconite (Wolfsbane).*
Misanthropy.	*Fuller's Teasel.*
Modest beauty	*Trillium Pictum.*
Modest genius	*Creeping Cereus.*
Modesty	*Violet.*
Modesty and purity	*White Lily.*
Momentary happiness	*Virginian Spiderwort.*
Mourning	*Weeping Willow.*
Music	*Bundles of Reed with their panicles.*
My best days are past	*Colchicum, or Meadow Saffron*
My regrets follow you to the grave . .	*Asphodel.*
Neatness	*Broom.*
Neglected beauty	*Throatwort.*
Never-ceasing remembrance . . .	*Everlasting.*
Old age	*Tree of Life.*
Only deserve my love	*Campion Rose.*
Painful recollections	*Flos Adonis.*
Painting	*Auricula.*
Painting the lily	*Daphne Odora.*
Passion.	*White Dittany.*
Paternal error	*Cardamine.*
Patience	*Dock. Ox Eye.*
Patriotism	*American Elm.*
Patriotism	*Nasturtium.*
Peace	*Olive.*
Perfected loveliness	*Camellia Japonica, White.*
Perfidy	*Common Laurel, in flower.*
Pensive beauty	*Laburnum.*
Perplexity	*Love in a Mist.*
Persecution	*Chequered Fritillary.*
Perseverance	*Swamp Magnolia.*
Persuasion	*Althea Frutex.*
Persuasion	*Syrian Mallow.*
Pertinacity	*Clotbur.*
Pity	*Pine.*
Pleasure and pain	*Dog Rose.*
Pleasure, lasting	*Everlasting Pea.*

Pleasures of memory	*White Periwinkle.*
Popular favour	*Cistus, or Rock Rose.*
Poverty	*Evergreen Clematis.*
Power	*Imperial Montague.*
Power	*Cress.*
Precaution	*Golden Rod.*
Prediction	*Prophetic Marigold.*
Pretension	*Spiked Willow Herb.*
Pride	*Amaryllis.*
Pride	*Hundred-leaved Rose.*
Privation	*Indian Plum.*
Privation	*Myrobalan.*
Profit	*Cabbage.*
Prohibition	*Privet.*
Prolific	*Fig Tree.*
Promptness	*Ten-week Stock.*
Prosperity	*Beech Tree.*
Protection	*Bearded Crepis.*
Prudence	*Mountain Ash.*
Pure love	*Single Red Pink.*
Pure and ardent love	*Double Red Pink.*
Pure and lovely	*Red Rosebud.*
Purity	*Star of Bethlehem.*
Quarrel	*Broken Corn-straw.*
Quicksightedness	*Hawkweed.*
Reason	*Goat's Rue.*
Recantation	*Lotus Leaf.*
Recall	*Silver-leaved Geranium.*
Reconciliation	*Filbert.*
Reconciliation	*Hazel.*
Refusal	*Striped Carnation.*
Regard	*Daffodil.*
Relief	*Balm of Gilead.*
Relieve my anxiety	*Christmas Rose.*
Religious superstition	*Aloe.*
Religious superstition	*Passion Flower.*
Religious enthusiasm	*Schinus.*
Remembrance	*Rosemary.*
Remorse	*Bramble.*
Remorse	*Raspberry.*
Rendezvous	*Chickweed.*
Reserve	*Maple.*
Resistance	*Tremella Nestoc.*
Restoration	*Persicaria.*
Retaliation	*Scotch Thistle.*
Return of happiness	*Lily of the Valley.*
Revenge	*Birdsfoot Trefoil.*
Reverie	*Flowering Fern.*

Reward of merit	*Bay Wreath.*
Reward of virtue.	*Garland of Roses.*
Riches	*Corn.*
Rigour	*Lantana.*
Rivalry.	*Rocket.*
Rudeness	*Clotbur.*
Rudeness	*Xanthium.*
Rural happiness	*Yellow Violet.*
Rustic beauty	*French Honeysuckle.*
Rustic oracle	*Dandelion.*
Sadness	*Dead Leaves.*
Safety	*Traveller's Joy.*
Satire	*Prickly Pear.*
Sculpture	*Hoya.*
Secret Love	*Yellow Acacia.*
Semblance	*Spiked Speedwell.*
Sensitiveness	*Mimosa.*
Sensuality	*Spanish Jasmine.*
Separation	*Carolina Jasmine.*
Severity	*Branch of Thorns.*
Shame	*Peony.*
Sharpness	*Barberry Tree.*
Sickness	*Anemone (Zephyr Flower).*
Silliness	*Fool's Parsley.*
Simplicity	*American Sweetbrier.*
Sincerity	*Garden Chervil.*
Slighted love	*Yellow Chrysanthemum.*
Snare	*Catchfly. Dragon Plant.*
Solitude	*Heath.*
Sorrow	*Yew.*
Sourness of Temper . . .	*Barberry.*
Spell	*Circæa.*
Spleen	*Fumitory.*
Splendid beauty	*Amaryllis.*
Splendour	*Austurtium.*
Sporting	*Fox-tail Grass.*
Stedfast Piety	*Wild Geranium.*
Stoicism	*Box Tree.*
Strength	*Cedar. Fennel.*
Submission	*Grass.*
Submission	*Harebell.*
Success crown your wishes . .	*Coronella.*
Succour	*Juniper.*
Sunbeaming eyes	*Scarlet Lychnis.*
Surprise	*Truffle.*
Susceptibility	*Wax Plant.*
Suspicion	*Champignon.*
Sympathy	*Balm.*
Sympathy	*Thrift.*

Talent	*White Pink.*
Tardiness	*Flax-leaved Goldy-locks.*
Taste	*Scarlet Fuchsia.*
Tears	*Helenium.*
Temperance	*Azalea.*
Temptation	*Apple.*
Thankfulness	*Agrimony.*
The colour of my fate	*Coral Honeysuckle.*
The heart's mystery	*Crimson Polyanthus.*
The perfection of female loveliness	*Justicia.*
The witching soul of music	*Oats.*
Thoughts	*Pansy.*
Thoughts of absent friends	*Zinnia.*
Thy frown will kill me	*Currant.*
Thy smile I aspire to	*Daily Rose.*
Ties	*Tendrils of Climbing Flants.*
Timidity	*Amaryllis.*
Timidity	*Marvel of Peru.*
Time	*White Poplar.*
Tranquillity	*Mudwort.*
Tranquillity	*Stonecrop.*
Tranquillize my anxiety	*Christmas Rose.*
Transient beauty	*Night-blooming Cereus.*
Transient impressions	*Withered White Rose.*
Transport of joy	*Cape Jasmine.*
Treachery	*Bilberry.*
True love	*Forget Me Not.*
True Friendship	*Oak-leaved Geranium.*
Truth	*Bittersweet Nightshade.*
Truth	*White Chrysanthemum.*
Unanimity	*Phlox.*
Unbelief	*Judas Tree.*
Unceasing remembrance	*American Cudweed.*
Unchanging friendship	*Arbor Vitæ.*
Unconscious beauty	*Burgundy Rose.*
Unexpected meeting	*Lemon Geranium.*
Unfortunate attachment	*Mourning Bride.*
Unfortunate love	*Scabious.*
Union	*Whole Straw.*
Unity	*White and Red Rose together.*
Unpatronized merit	*Red Primrose.*
Uselessness	*Meadowsweet.*
Utility	*Grass.*
Variety	*China Aster.*
Variety	*Mundi Rose.*
Vice	*Darnel (Ray Grass).*
Victory	*Palm.*
Virtue	*Mint.*

Virtue, Domestic	*Sage.*
Volubility	*Abecedary.*
Voraciousness	*Lupine.*
Vulgar Minds	*African Marigold.*
War	*York and Lancaster Rose.*
War	*Achillea Millefolia.*
Warlike trophy	*Indian Cress.*
Warmth of feeling	*Peppermint.*
Watchfulness	*Dame Violet.*
Weakness	*Moschatel.*
Weakness	*Musk Plant.*
Welcome to a stranger	*American Starwort.*
Widowhood	*Sweet Scabious.*
Win me and wear me	*Lady's Slipper.*
Winning grace	*Cowslip.*
Winter	*Guelder Rose.*
Wit	*Meadow Lychnis.*
Wit ill-timed	*Wild Sorrel.*
Witchcraft	*Enchanter's Nightshade*
Worth beyond beauty	*Sweet Alyssum.*
Worth sustained by judicious and tender affection	*Pink Convolvulus.*
Worthy all praise	*Fennel.*
You are cold	*Hortensia.*
You are my divinity	*American Cowslip.*
You are perfect	*Pine Apple.*
You are radiant with charms	*Ranunculus.*
You are rich in attractions	*Garden Ranunculus.*
You are the queen of coquettes	*Queen's Rocket.*
You have no claims	*Pasque Flower.*
You please all	*Branch of Currants.*
You will be my death	*Hemlock.*
Your charms are engraven on my heart	*Spindle Tree.*
Your looks freeze me	*Ice Plant.*
Your presence softens my pains	*Milkvetch.*
Your purity equals your loveliness	*Orange Blossoms.*
Your qualities, like your charms, are unequalled	*Peach.*
Your qualities surpass your charms	*Mignionette.*
Youthful innocence	*White Lilac.*
Youthful love	*Red Catchfly.*
Zealousness	*Elder.*
Zest	*Lemon.*

Language of Flowers.

DAFFODILS.

I WANDERED lonely as a cloud
 That floats on high o'er vales and hills,
When all at once I saw a crowd,
 A host of golden Daffodils;
Beside the lake, beneath the trees,
Fluttering and dancing in the breeze.

Continuous as the stars that shine
 And twinkle in the milky way,
They stretched in never-ending line
 Along the margin of a bay:
Ten thousand saw I at a glance,
Tossing their heads in sprightly dance.

The waves beside them danced; but they
 Outdid the sparkling waves in glee;
A poet could not but be gay,
 In such a jocund company;
I gazed and gazed, but little thought
What wealth the show to me had brought!

For oft when on my couch I lie,
 In vacant or in pensive mood,
They flash upon that inward eye
 Which is the bliss of solitude;
And then my heart with pleasure fills,
And dances with the Daffodils.

WORDSWORTH.

THE ROSE.

Go, lovely Rose!
Tell her that wastes her time on me,
 That now she knows,
When I resemble her to thee,
How sweet and fair she seems to be.

Tell her that's young,
And shuns to have her graces spied,
 That hadst thou sprung
In deserts where no men abide,
Thou must have uncommended died.

Small is the worth
Of beauty from the light retired;
 Bid her come forth,
Suffer herself to be desired,
And not blush so to be admired.

Then die, that she
The common fate of all things rare
 May read in thee;
How small a part of time they share
That are so wondrous sweet and fair.

Yet, though thou fade,
From thy dead leaves let fragrance rise
 And teach the maid
That goodness Time's rude hand defies;
That virtue lives when beauty dies.

WALLER.

THE SENSITIVE PLANT.

A Sensitive Plant in a garden grew,
And the young winds fed it with silver dew,
And it opened its fan-like leaves to the light,
And closed them beneath the kisses of Night.

*　　*　　*　　*　　*

But none ever trembled and panted with bliss
In the garden, the field, or the wilderness,
Like doe in the noontide with love's sweet want,
As the companionless Sensitive Plant.

The snowdrop, and then the violet,
Arose from the ground with warm rain wet,
And their breath was mixed with fresh odour, sent,
From the turf, like the voice and the instrument.

Then the pied wind-flowers and the tulip tall,
And narcissi, the fairest among them all,
Who gaze on their eyes in the stream's recess,
Till they die of their own dear loveliness.

And the naiad-like lily of the vale,
Whom youth makes so fair and passion so pale,
That the light of its tremulous bells is seen
Through their pavilions of tender green ;

And the hyacinth purple, and white, and blue,
Which flung from its bells a sweet peal anew
Of music so delicate, soft and intense,
It was felt like an odour within the sense !

And the rose like a nymph to the bath addrest,
Which unveiled the depth of her glowing breast,
Till, fold after fold, to the fainting air
The soul of her beauty and love lay bare ;

And the wand-like lily, which lifted up,
As a Mænad, its moonlight-coloured cup,
Till the fiery star, which is its eye,
Gazed through the clear dew on the tender sky;

And the jessamine faint, and the sweet tuberose,
The sweetest flower for scent that blows;
And all rare blossoms from every clime
Grew in that garden in perfect prime.

The Sensitive Plant, which could give small fruit
Of the love which it felt from the leaf to the root,
Received more than all [flowers], it loved more than ever,
Where none wanted but it, could belong to the giver—

For the Sensitive Plant has no bright flower;
Radiance and odour are not its dower;
It loves, even like Love its deep heart is full,
It desires what it has not, the beautiful!
*   *   *   *   *
Each and all like ministering angels were
For the Sensitive Plant sweet joy to bear,
Whilst the lagging hours of the day went by
Like windless clouds o'er a tender sky.

And when evening descended from heaven above,
And the earth was all rest, and the air was all love,
And delight, though less bright, was far more deep,
And the day's veil fell from the world of sleep,
*   *   *   *   *
The Sensitive Plant was the earliest
Up-gathered into the bosom of rest;
A sweet child weary of its delight,
The feeblest, and yet the favourite,
Cradled within the embrace of night.

SHELLEY.

O LUVE WILL VENTURE IN, &c.

TUNE—"*The Posie.*"

O LUVE will venture in, where it daur na weel be seen,
O luve will venture in, where wisdom ance has been ;
But I will down yon river rove, amang the wood sae green,
    And a' to pu' a posie to my ain dear May.

The primrose I will pu', the firstling o' the year,
And I will pu' the pink, the emblem o' my dear,
For she's the pink o' womankind, and blooms without a peer ;
    And a' to be a posie to my ain dear May.

I 'll pu' the budding rose, when Phœbus peeps in view,
For it 's like a baumy kiss o' her sweet bonnie mou ;
The hyacinth 's for constancy w' its unchanging blue,
    And a' to be a posie to my ain dear May.

The lily it is pure, and the lily it is fair,
And in her lovely bosom I 'll place the lily there ;
The daisy 's for simplicity and unaffected air,
    And a' to be a posie to my ain dear May.

The hawthorn I will pu', wi' its locks o' siller grey,
Where, like an aged man, it stands at break o' day,
But the songster's nest within the bush I winna tak away ;
    And a' to be a posie to my ain dear May.

The woodbine I will pu' when the e'ening star is near,
And the diamond-drops o' dew shall be her e'en sae clear :
The violet 's for modesty which weel she fa's to wear,
    And a' to be a posie to my ain dear May.

I 'll tie the posie round w' the silken band o' luve,
And I 'll place it in her breast, and I 'll swear by a' above,
That to my latest draught o' life the band shall ne'er remuve,
    And this will be a posie to my ain dear May.

BURNS.

MY NANNIE 'S AWA.

TUNE—"*There'll never be peace,*" *&c.*

Now in her green mantle blithe Nature arrays,
And listens the lambkins that bleat o'er the braes,
While birds warble welcome in ilka green shaw;
But to me it 's delightless—my Nannie 's awa.

The snaw-drap and primrose our woodlands adorn,
And violets bathe in the weet o' the morn;
They pain my sad bosom, sae sweetly they blaw,
They mind me o' Nannie—and Nannie 's awa.

Thou lav'rock that springs frae the dews of the lawn,
The shepherd to warn o' the grey-breaking dawn,
And thou mellow mavis that hails the night-fa',
Give over for pity— my Nannie 's awa.

Come, autumn, sae pensive, in yellow and grey,
And sooth me wi' tidings o' Nature's decay;
The dark, dreary winter, and wild-driving snaw,
Alane can delight me—now Nannie 's awa.

BURNS.

THEIR GROVES, &c.

TUNE—"*Humours of Glen.*"

THEIR groves o' sweet myrtle let foreign lands reckon,
  Where bright-beaming summers exalt the perfume;
Far dearer to me yon lone glen o' green breckan,
  Wi' the burn stealing under the lang yellow broom.

Far dearer to me are yon humble broom bowers,
  Where the blue-bell and gowan lurk lowly unseen;
For there, lightly tripping amang the wild flowers,
  A listening the linnet, aft wanders my Jean.

BURNS.

TO A MOUNTAIN DAISY,

On turning one down with a plough, in April 1786.

WEE, modest, crimson-tipped flow'r,
Thou's met me in an evil hour;
For I maun crush amang the stoure
          Thy slender stem ;
To spare thee now is past my pow'r,
          Thou bonnie gem.

Alas ! it's no thy neebor sweet,
The bonnie *Lark*, companion meet !
Bending thee 'mang the dewy weet !
          Wi' spreckled breast,
When upward-springing, blythe, to greet
          The purpling east.

Cauld blew the bitter-biting north
Upon thy early, humble birth ;
Yet cheerfully thou glinted forth
          Amid the storm,
Scarce rear'd above the parent earth
          Thy tender form.

The flaunting flow'rs our gardens yield,
High shelt'ring woods and wa's maun shield,
But thou beneath the random bield
          O' clod or stane,
Adorns the histie *stibble-field*,
          Unseen, alane.

There, in thy scanty mantle clad,
Thy snawy bosom sun-ward spread,
Thou lifts thy unassuming head
          In humble guise ;
But now the *share* uptears thy bed,
          And low thou lies !

Such is the fate of artless Maid,
Sweet *flow'ret* of the rural shade !
By love's simplicity betray'd,
          And guileless trust,
Till she, like thee, all soil'd, is laid
          Low i' the dust.

Such is the fate of simple Bard,
On life's rough ocean luckless starr'd !
Unskilful he to note the card
          Of *prudent lore*,
Till billows rage, and gales blow hard,
          And whelm him o'er !

Such fate to *suffering worth* is giv'n,
Who long with wants and woes has striv'n,
By human pride or cunning driv'n,
          To mis'ry's brink,
Till wrench'd of ev'ry stay but *Heav'n*,
          He, ruin'd, sink !

Ev'n thou who mourn'st the Daisy's fate,
That fate is thine—no distant date ;
Stern Ruin's *plough-share* drives, elate,
          Full on thy bloom,
Till crush'd beneath the furrow's weight,
          Shall be 'hy doom !

                  BURNS.

LAMENT OF MARY, QUEEN OF SCOTS.

On the Approach of Spring.

Now Nature hangs her mantle green
  On every blooming tree,
And spreads her sheets o' daisies white
  Out o'er the grassy lea;
Now Phœbus cheers the crystal streams,
  And glads the azure skies;
But nought can glad the weary wight
  That fast in durance lies.

Now lav'rocks wake the merry morn,
  Aloft on dewy wing;
The merle, in his noontide bow'r,
  Makes woodland echoes ring;
The mavis mild wi' many a note,
  Sings drowsy day to rest:
In love and freedom they rejoice,
  Wi' care nor thrall opprest.

Now blooms the lily by the bank,
  The primrose down the brae;
The hawthorn's budding in the glen,
  And milk-white is the slae;
The meanest hind in fair Scotland
  May rove their sweets amang;
But I, the Queen of a' Scotland,
  Maun lie in prison strang.

I was the Queen o' bonnie France,
  Where happy I hae been;
Fu' lightly rase I in the morn,
  As blythe lay down at e'en;
And I'm the sov'reign of Scotland,
  And mony a traitor there;
Yet here I lie in foreign lands,
  And never ending care.

But as for thee, thou false woman,
  My sister and my fae,
Grim vengeance, yet, shall whet a sword
  That thro' thy soul shall gae:
The weeping blood in woman's breast
  Was never known to thee;
Nor th' balm that draps on wounds of woe
  Frae woman's pitying e'e.

My son! my son! may kinder stars
  Upon thy fortune shine;
And may those pleasures gild thy reign,
  That ne'er wad blink on mine!
God keep thee frae thy mother's faes,
  Or turn their hearts to thee:
And where thou meet'st thy mother's friend,
  Remember him for me!

Oh! soon, to me, may summer-suns
  Nae mair light up the morn!
Nae mair, to me, the autumn winds
  Wave o'er the yellow corn!
And in the narrow house o' death
  Let winter round me rave;
And the next flow'rs that deck the spring,
  Bloom on my peaceful grave!

BURNS.

RED AND WHITE ROSES.

READ in these Roses the sad story
Of my hard fate, and your own glory ;
In the white you may discover
The paleness of a fainting lover ;
In the red the flames still feeding
On my heart with fresh wounds bleeding,
The white will tell you how I languish,
And the red express my anguish,
The white my innocence displaying,
The red my martyrdom betraying ;
The frowns that on your brow resided,
Have those roses thus divided.
Oh ! let your smiles but clear the weather,
And then they both shall grow together.

CAREW.

SONNET.

SWEET is the rose, but growes upon a brere ;
Sweet is the Juniper, but sharpe his bough ;
Sweet is the Eglantine, but pricketh nere ;
Sweet is the Firbloom, but his branches rough ;
Sweet is the Cypress, but his rind is tough,
Sweet is the Nut, but bitter is his pill ;
Sweet is the Broome-flowere, but yet sowre enough ;
And sweet is Moly, but his roote is ill.
So every sweet with sowre is tempred still,
That maketh it be coveted the more :
For easie things that may be got at will,
Most sorts of men doe set but little store.
Why then should I account of little pain,
That endless pleasure shall unto me gaine ?

SPENSER

TO PRIMROSES

FILLED WITH MORNING DEW.

Why do ye weep, sweet babes? Can tears
    Speak grief in you,
       Who were but born
       Just as the modest morn
     Teemed her refreshing dew?
Alas! ye have not known that shower
    That mars a flower:
       Nor felt the unkind
       Breath of a blasting wind;
     Nor are ye worn with years;
    Or warped as we,
     Who think it strange to see
Such pretty flowers, like to orphans young,
Speaking by tears before ye have a tongue.

Speak, whimpering younglings, and make known
    The reason why
       Ye droop and weep.
       Is it for want of sleep,
    Or childish lullaby?
Or that ye have not seen as yet
    The violet?
       Or brought a kiss
       From that sweetheart to this?
     No, no; this sorrow shown
    By your tears shed,
     Would have this lecture read:
That things of greatest, so of meanest worth,
Conceived with grief are, and with tears brought forth.

                    HERRICK.

A RED, RED ROSE.

Tune—" Wishaw's favourite."

O, MY luve's like a red, red rose,
   That's newly sprung in June :
O, my luve's like the melodie
   That's sweetly play'd in tune.

As fair art thou, my bonnie lass,
   So deep in luve am I ;
And I will luve thee still, my dear,
   Till a' the seas gang dry.

Till a' the seas gang dry, my dear,
   And the rocks melt w' the sun ;
I will luve thee still, my dear,
   While the sands o' life shall run.

And fare thee weel, my only luve !
   And fare thee weel a while ;
And I will come again, my luve,
   'Tho' it were ten thousand mile.

                                   BURNS.

VIRGINS promised when I died,
That they would each primrose-tide
Duly, morn and evening, come,
And with flowers dress my tomb.
—Having promised, pay your debts,
Maids, and here strew violets.

                        ROBERT HERRICK.

MUSIC, when soft voices die,
Vibrates in the memory ;
Odours when sweet violets sicken,
Love within the sense they quicken.

Rose leaves, when the rose is dead,
Are heaped for the beloved's bed ;
And so thy thoughts when thou art gone,
Love itself shall slumber on.

                              SHELLEY.

RADIANT sister of the day
Awake ! arise ! and come away !
To the wild woods and the plains,
To the pools where winter rains
Image all their roof of leaves,
Where the pine its garland weaves
Of sapless green, and ivy dun,
Round stems that never kiss the sun,
Where the lawns and pastures be
And the sandhills of the sea,
Where the melting hoar-frost wets
The daisy star that never sets,
And wind-flowers and violets
Which yet join not scent to hue
Crown the pale year weak and new :
When the night is left behind
In the deep east, dim and blind,
And the blue moon is over us,
And the multitudinous
Billows murmur at our feet,
Where the earth and ocean meet
And all things seem only one
In the universal sun.

                        P. B. SHELLEY.

TO DAFFODILS.

FAIR Daffodils, we weep to see
  You haste away so soon ;
As yet, the early-rising sun
  Has not attained its noon.
    Stay, stay,
  Until the hastening day
      Has run
  But to the even song ;
And having prayed together, we
  Will go with you along.

We have short time to stay as you,
  We have as short a spring ;
As quick a growth to meet decay,
  As you or any thing.
    We die,
  As your hours do, and dry
      Away,
  Like to the summer's rain,
Or as the pearls of morning's dew,
  Ne'er to be found again.

                    ROBERT HERRICK.

CONSTANCY.

LAY a garland on my hearse
Of the dismal yew ;
Maidens willow branches bear ;
Say, *I died true.*
My love was false, but I was firm
From my hour of birth.
Upon my buried body lie
Lightly, gentle earth !

                    SAMUEL FLETCHER.

MOURN, ilka grove the cushat kens !
Ye haz'lly shaws and briery dens !
Ye burnies, wimplin down your glens,
        Wi' toddlin din,
Or foaming strang, wi' hasty stens,
        Frae lin to lin.

Mourn little harebells o'er the lee ;
Ye stately foxgloves fair to see ;
Ye woodbines hanging bonnilie,
        In scented bow'rs ;
Ye roses on your thorny tree.
        The first o' flow'rs.

At dawn, when ev'ry grassy blade
Droops with a diamond at his head,
At ev'n, when beans their fragrance shed,
        I' th' rustling gale,
Ye maukins whiddin thro' the glade,
        Come join my wail.

Mourn, spring, thou darling of the year ;
Ilk cowslip cup shall kep a tear :
Thou, simmer, while each corny spear
        Shoots up its head,
Thy gay, green, flow'ry tresses shear,
        For him that's dead !

Thou, autumn, wi' thy yellow hair,
In grief thy sallow mantle tear !
Thou, winter, hurling thro' the air
        The roaring blast,
Wide o'er the naked world declare
        The worth we've lost !

                    BURNS.

TO THE SMALL CELANDINE.

PANSIES, Lilies, King-cups, Daisies,
Let them live upon their praises;
Long as there's a sun that sets,
    Primroses will have their glory;
Long as there are Violets,
    They will have a place in story;
There's a flower that shall be mine,
'Tis the little Celandine.

Ere a leaf is on the bush,
In the time before the thrush
Has a thought about her nest,
    Thou wilt come with half a call,
Spreading out thy glossy breast
Like a careless prodigal;
Telling tales about the sun,
When we've little warmth, or none.

Comfort have thou of thy merit,
Kindly unassuming spirit!
Careless of thy neighbourhood,
    Thou dost show thy pleasant face
On the moor, and in the wood,
    In the lane—there's not a place.
Howsoever mean it be,
But 'tis good enough for thee.

Ill befall the yellow flowers,
Children of the flaring hours!
Buttercups that will be seen,
    Whether we will see or no;
Others, too, of lofty mien,
    They have done as worldlings do.
Taken praise that should be thine,
Little, humble Celandine!

Prophet of delight and mirth,
Ill requited upon earth;
Herald of a mighty band,
    Of a joyous train ensuing,
Serving at my heart's command,
    Tasks that are no tasks renewing;
I will sing, as doth behove,
Hymns in praise of what I love!

WORDSWORTH.

TO BLOSSOMS.

FAIR pledges of a fruitful tree,
    Why do ye fall so fast?
    Your date is not so past,
But you may stay yet here awhile
    To blush and gently smile,
        And go at last.

What, were you born to be,
    An hour or half's delight,
    And so to bid good-night?
'Twas pity Nature brought ye forth,
    Merely to show your worth
        And lose you quite.

But you are lovely leaves, where we
    May read, how soon things have
    Their end, though ne'er so brave:
And after they have shown their pride,
    Like you, awhile, they glide
        Into the grave.

HERRICK.

72

THE LILY AND THE ROSE.

THE nymph must lose her female friend,
    If more admired than she—
But where will fierce contention end,
    If flowers can disagree.

Within the garden's peaceful scene
    Appear'd two lovely foes,
Aspiring to the rank of queen,
    The Lily and the Rose.

The Rose soon redden'd into rage,
    And, swelling with disdain,
Appeal'd to many a poet's page
    To prove her right to reign.

The Lily's height bespoke command,
    A fair imperial flower;
She seem'd designed for Flora's hand,
    The sceptre of her power.

This civil bick'ring and debate
    The goddess chanced to hear,
And flew to save, ere yet too late,
    The pride of the parterre.

Yours is, she said, the nobler hue,
    And yours the statelier mien;
And, till a third surpasses you,
    Let each be deemed a queen.

Thus, soothed and reconciled, each seeks
    The fairest British fair:
The seat of empire is her cheeks,
    They reign united there.

                    COWPER.

THE WALL-FLOWER.

WHY this flower is now called so,
List, sweet maids, and you shall know.
Understand this firstling was
Once a brisk and bonny lass,
Kept as close as Danae was,
Who a sprightly springald loved;
And to have it fully proved,
Up she got upon a wall,
'Tempting down to slide withal;
But the silken twist untied,
So she fell, and, bruised, she died.
Jove, in pity of the deed,
And her loving, luckless speed,
Turn'd her to this plant we call
Now "the flower of the wall."

                    HERRICK.

THE PRIMROSE.

ASK me why I send you here,
This firstling of the infant year;
Ask me why I send to you
This Primrose all bepearled with dew;
I straight will whisper in your ears,
The sweets of love are washed with tears.

Ask me why this flower doth show
So yellow, green, and sickly too;
Ask me why the stalk is weak
And bending, yet it doth not break;
I must tell you, these discover
What doubts and fears are in a lover.

                    CAREW.

ADONIS SLEEPING,

In midst of all, there lay a sleeping youth
Of fondest beauty. Sideway his face reposed
On one white arm, and tenderly unclosed,
By tenderest pressure, a faint damask mouth
To slumbery pout ; just as the morning south
Disparts a dew-lipp'd rose. Above his head,
Four lily stalks did their white honours wed
To make a coronal ; and round him grew
All tendrils green, of every bloom and hue,
Together intertwined and trammel'd fresh :
The vine of glossy sprout ; the ivy mesh,
Shading its Ethiop berries ; and woodbine,
Of velvet leaves, and bugle blooms divine.
                    Hard by,
Stood serene Cupids watching silently.
One, kneeling to a lyre, touch'd the strings,
Muffling to death the pathos with his wings ;
And, ever and anon, uprose to look
At the youth's slumber ; while another took
A willow bough, distilling odorous dew,
And shook it on his hair ; another flew
In through the woven roof, and fluttering-wise,
Rain'd violets upon his sleeping eyes.

Keats.

Modonna, wherefore hast thou sent to me
Sweet Basil and Mignonette,
Embleming love and health, which never yet
In the same wreath might be.
Alas, and they are wet !
Is it with thy kisses or thy tears ?
For never rain or dew
          Such fragrance drew
From plant or flower ; the very doubt endears
          My sadness ever new,
The sighs I breathe, the tears I shed, for thee.

P. B. Shelley.

THERE grew pied Wind-flowers and Violets,
Daisies, those pearl'd Arcturi of the earth,
The constellated flowers that never set ;
Faint Oxlips ; tender Blue-bells, at whose birth
The sod scarce heaved ; and that tall flower that wets
Its mother's face with Heaven-collected tears,
When the low wind, its playmate's voice, it hears.

And in the warm hedge grew lush Eglantine,
Green Cow-bind and the moonlight-colour'd May
And cherry blossoms, and white cups, whose wine
Was the bright dew yet drained not by the day :
And Wild Roses, and Ivy serpentine
With its dark buds and leaves, wandering astray,
And flowers azure, black, and streaked with gold,
Fairer than any wakened eyes behold.

And nearer to the river's trembling edge
There grew broad flag-flowers, purple prankt with white,
And starry river buds among the sedge,
And floating Water-lilies, broad and bright,
Which lit the oak that overhung the hedge
With moonlight beams of their own watery light ;
And bulrushes, and reeds of such deep green
As soothed the dazzled eye with sober sheen.

P. B. SHELLEY.

———————

FADE, Flow'rs ! fade, Nature will have it so ;
'Tis but what we must in our autumn do !
And as your leaves lie quiet on the ground,
The loss alone by those that lov'd them found ;
So in the grave shall we as quiet lie,
Miss'd by some few that lov'd our company ;
But some so like to thorns and nettles live,
That none for them can, when they perish, grieve.

WALLER.

ARRANGEMENT OF A BOUQUET.

HERE damask Roses, white and red,
    Out of my lap first take I,
Which still shall run along the thread,
    My chiefest flower this make I.

Amongst these Roses in a row,
    Next place I Pinks in plenty,
These double Pansies then for show ;
    And will not this be dainty ?

The pretty Pansy then I'll tie,
    Like stones some chain inchasing ;
And next to them, their near ally,
    The purple Violet placing.

The curious choice clove July flower,
    Whose kind hight the Carnation,
For sweetness of most sovereign power,
    Shall help my wreath to fashion ;

Whose sundry colours of one kind,
    First from one root derived,
Them in their several suits I'll bind :
    My garland so contrived.

A course of Cowslips then I'll stick,
    And here and there (though sparely)
The pleasant Primrose down I'll prick,
    Like pearls that will show rarely ;

Then with these Marigolds I'll make
    My garland somewhat swelling,
These Honeysuckles then I'll take,
    Whose sweets shall help their smelling.

The Lily and the Fleur-de-lis,
    For colour much contending :
For that I them do only prize,
    They are but poor in scenting.

The Daffodil most dainty is,
    To match with these in meetness ;
The Columbine compared to this,
    All much alike for sweetness.

These in their natures only are
    Fit to emboss the border,
Therefore I'll take especial care
    To place them in their order :

Sweet-williams, Campions, Sops-in-wine,
    One by another neatly ;
Thus have I made this wreath of mine,
    And finishéd it featly.

                        NICHOLAS DRAYTON.

THE CHERRY.

THERE is a garden in her face,
    Where roses and white lilies grow ;
A heavenly paradise is that place,
    Wherein all pleasant fruits do grow :
There cherries grow that none may buy
Till cherry ripe themselves do cry.

Those cherries fairly do enclose
    Of orient pearl a double row,
Which, when her lovely laughter shows,
    They look like rosebuds fill'd with snow ;
Yet them no peer nor prince may buy
Till cherry ripe themselves do cry.

Her eyes like angels watch them still,
    Her brows like bended bows do stand,
Threatening with piercing frowns to kill
    All that approach with eye or hand
These sacred cherries to come nigh,
Till cherry ripe themselves do cry.

                        RICHARD ALLISON

THE GARLAND.

THE pride of every grove I chose,
  The violet sweet and lily fair,
The dappled pink and blushing rose,
  To deck my charming Cloe's hair.

At morn the nymph vouchaf'd to place
  Upon her brow the various wreath;
The flowers less blooming than her face,
  The scent less fragrant than her breath.

The flowers she wore along the day;
  And every nymph and shepherd said,
That in her hair they look'd more gay
  Than glowing in their native bed.

Undrest, at ev'ning, when she found
  Their odours lost, their colours past;
She chang'd her look, and on the ground
  Her garland and her eye she cast.

That eye dropt sense distinct and clear,
  As any muse's tongue could speak,
When from its lid a pearly tear
  Ran trickling down her beauteous cheek.

Dissembling what I knew too well;
  My love! my life! said I, explain
This change of humour: pray thee tell:
  That falling tear.—What does it mean?

She sigh'd, she smil'd; and to the flowers
  Pointing, the lovely moralist said:
See! friend, in some few fleeting hours,
  See yonder, what a change is made!

Ah me! the blooming pride of May,
  And that of beauty are but one!
At morn both flourish bright and gay,
  Both fade at ev'ning, pale, and gone!

At dawn poor Stella danc'd and sung;
  The am'rous youth around her bow'd :
At night her fatal knell was rung!
  I saw and kiss'd her in her shroud :

Such as she is, who dy'd to-day,
  Such I, alas! may be to-morrow :
Go, Damon, bid thy muse display
  The justice of thy Cloe's sorrow.

PRIOR.

TO THE VIRGINS, TO MAKE
MUCH OF TIME.

GATHER ye rose-buds while ye may :
  Old Time is still a-flying ;
And this same flower that smiles to-day,
  To-morrow will be dying.

The glorious lamp of heaven, the sun,
  The higher he's a-getting,
The sooner will his race be run,
  And nearer he's to setting.

That age is best, which is the first,
  When youth and blood are warmer ;
But being spent, the worse and worst
  Times will succeed the former.

—Then be not coy, but use your time,
  And while ye may, go marry ;
For having lost but once your prime,
  You may for ever tarry.

ROBERT HERRICK.

SONG OF MAY MORNING.

Now the bright morning-star, day's harbinger,
Comes dancing from the east, and leads with her
The flowery May, who from her green lap throws
The yellow cowslip, and the pale primrose.
  Hail, bounteous May, that dost inspire
  Mirth, and youth, and warm desire;
  Woods and groves are of thy dressing,
  Hill and dale doth boast thy blessing.
Thus we salute thee with our early song,
  And welcome thee, and wish thee long.

MILTON.

AMONG the myrtles as I walk'd,
Love and my Sight thus intertalk'd:
Tell me, said I, in deep distress,
Where I may find my Shepherdess?
—Thou Fool, said Love, know'st thou not this?
In everything that's sweet she is.
In yon'd Carnation go and seek,
There thou shalt find her lips and cheek;
In that enamell'd Pansy by,
There thou shalt have her curious eye;
In bloom of Peach and Rose's bud
There waves the streamer of her blood.
—'Tis true, said I; and thereupon
I went to pluck them one by one,
To make of parts an unión;
But on a sudden all were gone.
At which I stopp'd; said Love, these be
The true resemblance of Thee;
For as these Flowers, thy joys must die;
And in the turning of an eye;
And all thy hopes of her must wither,
Like those short sweets here knit together.

ROBERT HERRICK.

FRAGMENT, IN WITHERSPOON'S
COLLECTION OF SCOTCH SONGS.

TUNE—"*Hughie Graham.*"

" O GIN my love were yon red rose,
 "That grows upon the castle wa' ;
" And I mysel' a drap o' dew,
 " Into her bonnie breast to fa' !

" Oh, there beyond expression blest,
 " I'd feast on beauty a' the night ;
" Seal'd on her silk-saft faulds to rest,
 " Till fley'd awa by Phœbus' light."

*O were my love yon lilac fair,
 Wi' purple blossoms to the spring ;
And I, a bird to shelter there,
 When wearied on my little wing :

How I wad mourn, when it was torn
 By autumn wild, and winter rude !
But I wad sing on wanton wing,
 When youthfu' May its bloom renew'd.*

---

* These stanzas were added by BURNS.

THE DAISY.

OF all the floures in the mede
Than love I most these floures white and rede
Soch that men callen Daisies in our town,
To hem I have so great affection,
As I sayd erst, when comen is the Maie,
That in my bedde there daweth me no daie,
That I n'am up and walking in the mede
To see this floure ayenst the Sunne sprede ;
Whan it up riseth early by the morrow,
That blissful sight softeneth all my sorrow.

       CHAUCER.

ILLUSTRATIONS.

—:o:—